STEVE RUSH

Improov Publishing, United Kingdom

Published in the United Kingdom by:
Improov Publishing
Lalstone House,
22 Maes Y Gwenyn
Vale of Glamorgan
CF62 3LA
www.leadershipcake.com

Leadership Cake copyright © 2013 Steve Rush
First printed October 2013
Content edited and designed by Tanya Brockett, Hallagen Ink
Cover designed by Ben Steer, Inov8 Design

ISBN: 978-0-9927127-0-9
ISBN: 978-0-9927127-1-6 (ePub e-book)
ISBN: 978-0-9927127-2-3 (PDF e-book)

This book is dedicated to all of the great (and not so great) leaders I have had; to my fantastic wife Claire; and to my children: Charlie, Harry, Ellie and Hudson—who are leading and inspiring my future.

Contents

Preface

Leadership.

"Here we go," I hear you cry, "another book on leading people and teams."

I understand that for many of you having any length of experience in leading others and teams, there are so many models, philosophies and structures you could follow, it is challenging to decide which one is the right one.

My approach is very simple: In my twenty-two years of leading people, from small teams to large global businesses, the "many models" approach is a good one. This means that no one model on its own will suffice, but you should take elements from as many models as you can to help you define your thinking.

My research and experience tells me that it is not about the model, nor is it about the role, the organization, or the task, but it is about whether the individual who "LEADS" that team has all the necessary ingredients. It is also about mixing those leadership ingredients in the right quantity to be the most effective and successful leader he or she can be.

The leaders I have worked with, when asked, "what is it that makes you a leader," generally did not identify with any specific characteristics, traits or styles that led to their leadership career. In most cases, their leadership experience had emerged from their life and work experiences both consciously and subconsciously. Without fail I used to hear, "I wish I'd had a recipe for success years ago."

This book explores the principle that leadership is created just like a cake; it's a whole creation, born out of a list of ingredients, all of which are essential to create the perfect cake. The cake is a metaphor for you, and the ingredients and construction are you and your style. Our recipe will help you become a great leader.

Get your ingredients, mixing and baking right, and you are a great leader; get them wrong and you (and your *Cake*) can taste awful.

Introduction

It was a cold and crisp Sunday morning in November. My wife and I were relaxing in bed just chatting through our planned events of the day. As many attentive husbands do, I was attempting a deep conversation with my wife, but at the same time I was trying to think about the coaching interventions that I had partly completed the week before and still had playing on my mind. I was due to continue the meeting the following morning.

My lovely wife Claire comes from a traditional family in the north of England. She is a stickler for keeping hold of traditions and is also keen to pass on those customs to our children. She was explaining to me the tradition of "Stir-up Sunday."

Stir-up Sunday is an informal term for the last Sunday before the season of Advent where she would ask all of the family to add an ingredient into a bowl and in turn stir these ingredients to make the perfect Christmas cake. This way, come Christmas day, the cake and its ingredients will have blended together and matured perfectly.

Picture the scene: I'm thinking dysfunctional leader ... mixed up approach with their team ... some overplayed strengths that are now limitations, etc. In the background, Claire is embellishing the story of Stir-up Sunday.

Then I suddenly hear and connect with the words, "if you don't get the ingredients spot on, measured perfectly from my recipe, it won't be right, it won't taste as it should, and in fact, it won't be a Christmas cake at all."

With that I leapt startled from the bed, "That's it ... cake," I proclaimed. *"Leadership Cake!"*

She was a little confused I have to tell you. "What on earth are you going on about," she cried.

I preached, "The recipe to be a great leader: all leaders need a recipe for their *Leadership Cake*.

In fact, if their ingredients aren't right, or mixed well, their cake is not a *Leadership Cake*."

So thank you, Claire, for the inspiration, and I apologize for being distracted, but *Leadership Cake* was born on Stir-up Sunday.

1 *Recipe for "Cake"*

Where Can I Find My Leadership Recipe?

In this book, I will explore with you the concept of "you" as a leader and what you need to possess to be a great leader. We will also discover what to avoid and how to build and develop greatness in your leadership career. The stories I share will raise your awareness to some of your personal attributes that could work for you and also against you if you overplay them.

We will do this together, thinking about "cake" as a metaphor for you. *Leadership Cake*—full

1

of the freshest, well balanced and thought through ingredients: baked to perfection and palatable to all those who experience you, crumbs and all.

So, let's think about "cake." I'm no baking expert, so in order to make the near perfect cake, where would I start? A cookbook maybe? Well, certainly I would suggest you look up a recipe.

When it comes to creating a recipe for leadership, there are about as many ideas as there are cookbooks for cakes, but there are some core ingredients in our *Leadership Cake* that you can't do without.

Every cake needs flour, eggs, sugar and butter; otherwise it's not a cake, right? Just as if you were baking a real cake, you can't leave out the core ingredients in your *Leadership Cake*. We will discuss our *Leadership Cake* ingredients later, but where do we find the recipe so we at least know what to put into it?

I have experienced leadership in action and when it works and when it does not. The recipe for success can often be found within our experience and those who were leaders before us.

My mother has a recipe for cake that my wife and children use today. It has been passed down over generations and adapted and modified based on experience, access to newer ingredients and the change in one's palate. It's also true that people's taste and expectations may have been modified over time.

Leaders of the nineteenth century may today be viewed as archaic dictators. There are leaders who we may have looked up to twenty years ago. Without updating their ingredients, however, they may now seem outdated and stale.

If you have been dependent on a certain cookbook, it may well determine what your *"Cake"* tastes like. As bakers we want our recipients to enjoy cake. Bakers want to get feedback that their cake was pleasing to the palate. As leaders we want our outcomes and results to be received in the same way, particularly with how we operate or lead our people and businesses.

When I work with business leaders and teams, there are many names shared that are synonymous with being great leaders. Here are a few that are at the forefront of people's minds:

Mahatma Gandhi was born an ordinary chap with strong determination to be great at whatever he did. After completing a law degree from London, he became the most important part of the Indian struggle for freedom from the British colonial rule. His policy of non-violent protest through civil disobedience and unrest eventually succeeded when he led his country to independence in 1947.

The most notable ingredients in his *Leadership Cake* were: resilience, knowledge, people-skills, motivation, and communication. His approach to leading was "by example."

Winston Churchill was Prime Minister of Britain from 1940 to 1945. He led Great Britain against Nazi Germany during World War II. He worked well with the allies and consequently defeated the regime of Hitler.

Churchill's *Leadership Cake* was made up of: fearlessness, authenticity, determination, empathy, unyielding perseverance and undying devotion to his goal.

Jack Welch was an American chemical engineer, business executive, and author. He was Chairman and CEO of General Electric (GE) between 1981 and 2001. During his time at GE, the company's value rose four thousand percent. Jack's *Leadership Cake* was full of: energy, edge, execution, passion, knowledge, and communication. This provided his leadership team with an ongoing legacy.

Richard Branson is the founder and chairman of Virgin Group. The Group has grown from a music mail order business in 1970 to one of the most recognized and successful brands of all time, with four hundred companies under his leadership. Richard's *Leadership Cake* consists of: a healthy dollop of vision, courage, authenticity, discipline, motivation, communication and empathy for his staff and clients.

Bill Gates is chairman of Microsoft and is cited as the leader of the personal computer revolution. In his early career, it was reported that his leadership style was very combative, but after changing his ingredients and rethinking in his *Leadership Cake*, he became more collaborative, created a culture of restless curiosity, and used his knowledge, communication and desire to achieve.

As you can see from the five leaders that I have shared, there are lots of different ingredients in the making of *Leadership Cake*. The ingredients shift a little from individual to individual, but all have a track record of achievement based on their leadership styles or how they created their *Leadership Cake*.

There are many other leaders who have shone brightly in their business and personal achievements—you indeed may have worked with them in your past careers. If you consider any leader that has created the right environment for success, there are some common ingredients.

Is there such thing as the perfect leader or perfect *Leadership Cake*? Of course not! We are all susceptible to emotion, thinking and feelings, and as such, we cannot be robotic in our actions. When faced with certain circumstances or events in our lives, we react. Our reaction will dictate our outcome to any event, so understanding what ingredients mix well with others is an essential element in baking the right kind of *Leadership Cake*.

Often we don't understand what ingredients our leaders actually have; what we experience is their reaction to events—or how their *Cake* tastes in different situations.

There is a great equation that I learned from Jack Canfield, author of *The Success Principles*, which is:

$$E + R = O$$

E + R = O. The "E" is for **E**vents; they are just things that happen. As leaders, it is our **R**esponse to those events that determines the resulting **O**utcome.

Our ingredients (beliefs, values, habits, etc.) lead to our Response. The Event can be the same for many leaders, but the balance of their ingredients will determine their Response, and thus, their Outcomes. Understanding the ingredients to leadership will help us identify those that are present in those leading us.

In our *Leadership Cake*, I will refer to the models, insights and finer ingredients shared as "condiments."

So let's explore the essential, must-have ingredients and condiments.

2 *Four Essential Ingredients for Cake*

My mother uses a simple recipe that is generations old in our family. Growing up around her, the art of weights and measures was commonplace in the kitchen. Like all good cooks, she had adapted her cake mix to be the most effective yet simple to follow so she could deliver a great cake experience. She did so naturally and effortlessly without too much thought after time.

Because we are thwarted by lots of tasks, actions, people to manage and to lead as leaders, I want to break down the key essential ingredients. There are four essential leadership ingredients. While these are essential, they are not the only four, however, without them it's not a *Cake*.

C - Communication
A - Authenticity
K - Knowledge
E - Empathy

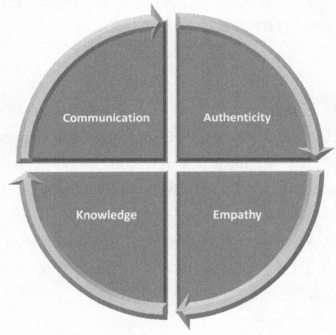

Recipe tip—Mix the ingredients together well. Be sure to blend your ingredients in a large bowl and whisk until consistent to ensure the perfect base to your *Cake*. Add flavoring according to taste.

Communication

When you look at some of the world's greatest leaders, one common ingredient they share is that they are all exceptional communicators. They have the ability to convey a message and resonate and engage deeply with their audience consistently.

The irony is that it is often the case that we are not taught to be great communicators during our early years. Early communication is a learned behavior taught to us by people around us, such as parents and siblings.

If they were good communicators, there is a likelihood of us being good communicators.

At school, we are taught grammar, punctuation, pronunciation and vocabulary. If we were confident individuals, we may have been asked to share that in class, but all of the above just teaches us one approach: It teaches communication that focuses on what we do.

The greatest communicators in leadership have a sixth sense that also focuses on what others may do and how they do it while interpreting the reasons why.

I call these individuals "Communication Adaptors." They have the ability in the blink of an eye to adapt their style, pace or tone to vary the message based not on their message, but based on the person or group with whom they are communicating.

Have you ever tried having a conversation with somebody and they were just not responsive? The answer may lie in the way you were communicating with them.

When I have worked with leaders who were also communication adaptors, it was almost certain that they had less awkward or less confrontational experiences and dialogue. This was because they worked their communication skills with their recipient in mind. By adopting this approach, the recipient responded more positively and the leader's personal message was delivered more effectively.

There are other things at play in effective communication, of course. The following areas (or condiments) are to help raise your awareness as to how you communicate or how you are perceived as a communicator.

Be Clear

While leading a team of senior managers, I was struggling to get a consistent performance and close performance results for people in my business area. On a wet Wednesday while reflecting over a stiff Americano, I suddenly realized that my communication style had an enemy—this enemy is called ambiguity.

One of the baking methods of great communication is to get rid of ambiguity. Be really clear why you do what you do and what's expected of people. Being this thoughtful as to my outcomes helped me develop the clarity to say and demonstrate how I was going to produce results.

I developed the following model by accident, but it transformed my results and improved revenue significantly year on year.

Standards—Expectations—Consequences (S.E.C.)

Standards—Be crystal clear by communicating what your standards are with your team or business. What should their individual behaviors be? What results would constitute them meeting standard? What is their role in developing their people? How, what and when will they spend time training themselves or others and how does this support the business, their clients and their staff?

Also communicate why, or what I now refer to as "the reasons" that it is important to them or the business. In my time as a consultant, understanding context helps create buy-in to any process or initiative.

If your employees fundamentally understand "why" or "the reasons" they are doing what they are doing, then their buy-in and motivation are significantly improved from the outset.

This building block is essential to ensure that people really do understand what you expect—then be restless every day to ensure that your team is working as close as it can to these standards with your support.

Expectations—First the "Whys" and "What fors" and now the "Hows." How will you behave and communicate with all of the people, clients and stakeholders that you interact with? How will you deliver the results? How will you support your top performing staff and clients? Who else is involved and when would you expect to see action take place to deliver what you expect? Your focus should not be limited to those who respond well to your leadership. You should also consider how you develop your less productive relationships.

Let's not forget the importance of communicating this effectively and ensuring that everyone has received the message. We explore how we know it's been received a little later in this chapter.

It's important for us to consider that this is not about telling. This is about showing your people how, your reasons, when and what you expect; this should be delivered by you with conviction in an effective clear and communicative way.

Consequences—I call this, "what if you do & what if you don't." It's really important that you describe to all people in your organization regardless of their seniority what the journey will be like specifically for them. If they meet your standards and expectations, how will the benefits of delivering a shared vision be linked to their personal achievements?

Conversely, if we don't spend enough time communicating honestly with people from the outset about the consequences of not meeting these standards and expectations, our old enemy ambiguity could revisit us once more. Nobody likes surprises, right?

I have often overheard conversations of leaders saying, "it's a bit of tough love." This doesn't need to be tough love. It could be good old-fashioned honest communication, with a teaspoonful of restless curiosity to make sure your staff adheres to your Standards, Expectations and Consequences.

Stir in a pinch of zero tolerance for mediocrity and this model will help you shine above your competitors.

By communicating S.E.C. effectively, you will build great morale, and staff will energize each other. While productivity grows, you will foster a strong personal brand reputation for leading others. This will all be because you have successfully communicated "clarity."

Getting on their Agenda

This is another method of communicating with a clear goal of drawing out positive behavior. Being on their agenda develops a fundamental understanding of the individual you are working with.

There is an old saying: "give to receive." The philosophy behind this phrase assumes that by communicating openly and getting on the agenda of others, you will receive a more productive reaction in whatever you do.

As leaders, you need to know what is going on at every level, right? As leaders, a primary role should be asking curious questions at every department level, in other words "fact finding." However, if you fact find with the genuine intent of helping others achieve their goals and aspirations, you will not only open your window to any given situation, but also help build trust, affinity and gather business crucial insight.

A most important fact is that you will learn a huge amount about that individual by the way they communicate with you, or not, as the case may be.

Two Way or the Highway

Communication has to be two way, i.e., one person sending a message and the other responding, otherwise it's not communicating.

Many of the leaders I work with have time pressures. I understand that busy people have to get the message out timely and efficiently. If you don't get a response, how can you be sure you have actually communicated?

What you can be sure of is that you have simply "cascaded and shared a flow of information." If you use communication methods such as conference calls and webinars to send a message or information to a wider audience, ask yourself, "How can I be sure they have received my communication?"

Keeping it interactive is essential. You can keep communication flowing both ways and ensure people are listening with a pert ear by throwing the odd testing question out there. A favorite of mine is nominating ad-hoc presenters of the subject matter to ensure everybody is engaged with any supporting slides or messages.

To consolidate their learning and to test if I had communicated, I often found it useful to ask them to follow up with a confirmation e-mail of the three things they will do as a result of the communication. This way you can test it. (This only works if you follow it up! If you don't, you have lost impact the next time you try.)

Finally, if you do use telephone conference calls, have you ever recorded yourself? Try playing "you" back... some interesting reflection and observations about your communication style can be learned in doing this.

Look and Listen

Great leaders have perfected the art of observing communication in the unspoken word, body language, idiosyncrasies, and behaviors. You do not have to be a NLP practitioner to use your instinct and intuition.

Neuro-linguistic programming (NLP) is a communication approach that is fast becoming a science between consultants, coaches and psychotherapists. NLP was the brainchild of Richard Bandler and John Grinder in California during the 1970s.

Bandler and Grinder claim there is connection between the neurological processes (N), how and what we say, our language (L), and the behavioral patterns and gestures we subconsciously program (P). Their practice suggests that through these three triggers, our experiences can be read and interpreted. A practitioner of NLP can demonstrate a strong understanding of these principles

There have been many investigations into "gut reaction." What appears to be counter-intuitive is overwhelmingly accurate when tested.

There have been numerous studies that have found that individuals who used their intuition and instinct based on what they were observing were more often right than they are wrong. Some research suggests that gut reaction could be as much as 80% accurate.

To be a great communicator you can be more effective belly button to belly button if you master the art of non-verbal communication.

It's well documented that non-verbal communication can be at least 55% of any sent message, but what you also need is the ability to listen with precision to capture the other 45% (which itself is made up of 7% words and 38% tone).

How you say something can be significantly more important than what you say. Try reading this next sentence out to a colleague:

"You said she stole my watch."

Now ask that same colleague, "What did I tell you about?" Your response will be varied based on how you said it! There are actually six statements here and based on the emphasis, tone and pitch change on each word, the sentence takes on a new meaning. Try it out.

Have you ever had a conversation when you have found yourself saying, "No, that's not what I meant," or "I'm not sure you heard me." The chances are that it may have been how you delivered your message.

A Spoonful Too Much of Communication

We will now explore what happens when you don't get the right quantities of your *Leadership Cake* mix: your *Cake* will not taste as good as it should. It may be too sweet or too bitter, and just one small amount of extra core ingredient could spoil your intended outcome of the *Leadership Cake* you are looking to bake.

Your "C" or communication is a significant ingredient in your *Cake* mix. As a leader, what, how, when and the reasons you communicate a message represents not only you but the wider corporate strategy too.

I have worked with leaders who have stated, "this company doesn't know what it's doing." Frequently, after discussion, we establish what they were really saying was, "my boss hasn't told me or engaged me in what the organization wants to achieve and how I fit in to the plan." Or, "I do not understand."

CASE STUDY John is recognized as a successful business leader. Having developed his career over many years, he has been recognized as strong and versatile. He has a track record of delivering results.

John's *Cake* mixture appears to have been sound.

Recently, the board increased the challenge to John to improve output and results. John went overboard letting his direct reports and staff know exactly what they need to do and how they should go about it.

John is expecting everybody in his business area to work extra hours to meet the board's challenge. He has also taken the view to meet with his senior team daily and every two days he is having a telephone conference call with the junior managers to ensure they felt the same urgency as their boss.

In addition to this, he has created a whole new reporting process in which his business area managers are required to send results, by return e-mail, to his office twice a day.

John had a perception that by increasing urgency and communication, he will get a snap in results as he had seen other leaders adopt a similar approach.

He's right of course; he will get a short-term shift in results by increasing the urgency. The chances of him sustaining longer-term consistent performance is unlikely, however, because his *Cake* mixture has a spoonful too much of communication and the other ingredients are overpowered.

By over communicating, he will reduce his impact. By merely relying on his knowledge, he fundamentally felt that it was the right thing to do, but eventually he will lose communication impact. This also has an impact on his authenticity, as it is a copied process that demonstrates little empathy to co-workers' commitments, existing workload and other activities. As a result, John's *Cake* tastes different.

His team doesn't have a well-balanced *Cake* and they know it, however they probably don't understand why that is... or the reasons.

A Spoonful Too Few of Communication

CASE STUDY Mary is new to her leadership role and has been leading a large business for ten years. She has recently been appointed by her company to lead the largest distribution channel. During her first few weeks, Mary decided to spend her time getting to know the business and understand the issues and opportunities her new business offered.

After one week she met with her senior managers and spent a significant amount of time getting to know them and sharing her knowledge. Shortly after her third week, she introduced a weekly communication that shared her thoughts with the wider workforce to help raise their awareness.

Mary also introduced a monthly telephone meeting with all of her direct reports to share information to enable them to focus on the job at hand and not become distracted.

After several months, Mary was concerned that results and revenue were not traveling in the right direction, so she introduced a weekly meeting template. Mary called this a "pulse check." This would provide her with key management information about which she could discuss on her monthly conference calls with her team. Results didn't move much despite her intervention.

All of Mary's actions to help her to understand the business and her people were created with great intention. How effective a communicator was she? On the face of it, Mary appears to have communicated well, however, if we examine her approach, Mary did not communicate enough.

A leader's role, when they are new to a business, is to provide a vision and a shared goal. This is so all of their staff at whatever level can be an integral part of the journey. That was absent from Mary's *Cake* right?

Mary was not clear. Even though she was structured about setting out her expectations, she never tested that the whole of the business understood what it was she was actually trying to achieve.

Mary didn't deliver communication to a consistent and meaningful level. She had some good ideas, but as Mary's *Cake* had a spoonful too few of communication, the other ingredients could overpower this recipe. She had attempted to be truly authentic by sharing her depth of knowledge and getting to understand her people and their objectives. She was not able to communicate effectively as she relied on cascade and remote communication too much.

As we established earlier, up to 55% of Mary's communication opportunity had gone untested and unmeasured. The lack of "why, the reasons, what, how and when" could have been overshadowed or even missed. There was not enough breadth in her communication strategy.

Mary's *Leadership Cake* just doesn't taste right. Her team doesn't have a well-balanced *Cake* and they know it, but they probably don't understand why that is.

* * * *

Getting a measure of your communication in your *Leadership Cake* will help you mirror some of the great communication from leaders we shared earlier. If you don't put enough flour in your cake or put too much, it will spoil your cake, as the best chefs will tell you.

In your *Leadership Cake* mixture, too much or too little ... then it's not a *Cake*. It may look like a *Cake* (or a leader), but it will not taste like one.

Take a moment to reflect on your communication style as a leader and use the recipe pad on the following page to fine tune your "C" Communication ingredients. Make sure you "add according to taste" what you need, and "leave out" where you believe it may overpower your Cake.

Recipe Pad
"C" Communication

Add in ...

Leave out ...

Authenticity

Communication is essential to help your authenticity. So is authenticity a choice? Is it a trait? I don't think so. It's also not a learned behavior. Can you imagine having to provide feedback following a meeting with a colleague by asking them, "I'd like it if you could try to be more authentic, please?"

Quite simply put, authentic behavior in leadership means unique or original. One of the easiest ways to mess up your *Cake* is by trying to sound or behave like somebody else or by mimicking a co-worker.

Authenticity is another core ingredient in our *Leadership Cake* mixture. Bill George's book called, *Authentic Leadership: Rediscovering the Secrets to Creating Lasting Value* (2003), provided new thinking and suggested that authentic leaders were more effective. Being authentic means you should avoid mimicking others, but at the same time, what this does not suggest is that you should not learn from one another. Capturing and sharing great ideas and modeling the right behavior shapes who we become. It's important that we learn from those around us and model good skills and behaviors in other leaders.

Leaders became good leaders and good leaders became great leaders by learning "how to" from all of their interactions with people, in particular those leaders who inspired and motivated them.

What makes authentic leaders stand out in the *Leadership Cake* shop is that everything they do, they actually believe in it wholeheartedly. They also demonstrate conviction in everything they say. This is all delivered with humility.

When leaders physically demonstrate humility and belief in what they say and do, they create instant trust and belief with their people, stakeholders and clients. If their followers didn't believe what they said and did, it would smell like a ten-week old gateau. We are simple and social human beings and we are programmed to smell rotten *Cake* from a cake stand a mile away.

We sometimes just get that feeling that we can't quite put our finger on, but we know it's not right! And that's because our instinct tells us that our leader or people who are attempting to influence us are not being authentic.

Being authentic is a key ingredient in your *Leadership Cake*. Demonstrating authenticity to people who work with you will allow them the security to trust your judgment. They will support your vision and work for you as well as themselves.

Direct reports of authentic leaders even put up with their failures for no other reason than they trust their judgment. After all, your success as a leader is all about them delivering what you expect, right?

Here are some candy sprinkles for your "A" in *Cake*:

(s + d) x B = A

If you *Say* and *Do* what you genuinely *Believe*, you are *Authentic*.

Let's look at other benefits and traits of authenticity (or flavorings for your *Cake*). This should help raise your awareness.

Trust—It's something I've blogged about previously via social media (such as Twitter and LinkedIn) and had great responses and interesting discussion. It's easy to "trust" somebody because it's a choice you make. It is your decision to trust that individual or not; you make that final call.

Some people need more evidence than others to make a decision about trust, but let's flip that scenario. For you to be trusted, it's you that needs to provide the evidence. As we have just learned, by actually demonstrating a belief in what you do, why you do it and how you say it, this alone will lead people to trust in you.

All trusted leaders are prepared to give of themselves. If you are prepared to give yourself to

LEADERSHIP CAKE

your staff, you will be more open to those you work with. The more they see and hear of you and understand that your intentions are honorable and genuine, the more they will trust you. The better the trust, the more authentic you can become.

Fairness is a sub-ingredient of trust, if you always do what's right and fair (people sometimes may not like it), they will almost definitely trust your judgment. As easy as it is to build trust, it's as easy to lose it.

Just one broken promise, a corporate white lie, not doing what you said you would do, will erode trust. Once you have let trust slip through people's hands, it's very hard to recover. Without trust underpinning your authenticity as a leader, you will become a very vanilla *Cake* at best, and you will struggle at every juncture to engage people and deliver what's required, other than the basics.

Integrity—It's an ingredient on every leader's CV (curriculum vitae), even if it's not in their *Cake*. It's a very easy thing to say, "I have integrity," however, it is much more difficult in

36

leadership to actually display it. Where do you find it? Where did you learn about it? How do you know you've really got it? If you look up integrity in a dictionary, you'll probably find descriptors like: "adhering to moral and ethical principles or soundness of moral character." Nice words right?

I have been in boardrooms far too many times to recall where some of these descriptors get left behind in the pursuit of a corporate career or success. Ironically, without integrity, you will struggle to get people to trust you in the first place, and of course, that may add doubt to your authenticity.

How many leaders do you know where maybe in passing you've heard, "I know it's not right," "I don't get it?" "Let's just do it, we need to keep the business happy." What about doing what's right to keep the business happy and if you don't get it—challenge it?

As soon as you leave the boardroom, the messages and direction you give becomes your business message as a leader. If you don't get it and you think it's not right, then your staff and clients rely on you to challenge it. Being brave and voicing your concerns in a measured, structured and unemotional way can help demonstrate that you are acting with integrity.

I do understand you sometimes have to have a political approach when you are dealing with your seniors in corporate society, board members, peers and stakeholders, but you can still be commercially and politically sensitive and at the same time display integrity!

If politicians did not have some integrity, nothing for the greater good would get done and nobody would vote for them. It's easy to spot any individual's lack of integrity and you can see they are not authentic because what they are saying and doing don't add up in what they are telling you they believe.

Buy in—If you are authentic, trusted and your integrity is high, you get buy in. You need the people working with you to share your vision and make commitments to the cause. This includes stakeholders, staff, peers and your family. I want to share a brief story that demonstrates this.

I was leading a significant business unit turning over $850 million a year in new sales, which was a stretch on previous performance. I was provided with revenue and budget targets for the next six months that appeared unrealistic on first glance. Once I'd worked through my deployment, resourcing and tactics along with strong leadership from my senior team, I genuinely felt we could deliver what was asked.

I provided my senior members with their teams' objectives and showed them based on my rudimentary calculations that this task was realistic and achievable.

I had already invested a lot of effort with my staff by this time, saying and doing what I believed, subsequently these guys had my back when I needed them because I'd always had theirs.

They assembled their teams to plan. A short while later they returned. On this occasion they had collectively achieved the same results with their teams as I had intended with them. The results we were broadly now forecasting as a business unit were even higher than our initial challenge. Later that week, I stood in front of my fellow directors and peers at a conference, along with all of their reports, and shared our business unit's vision.

This was received by my fellow colleagues with aghast, disbelief, and indeed, one of my fellow directors thought it was so unlikely we would achieve it, he shouted, "Next interesting headline: red bus found on the moon!"

Needless to say, I enjoyed the heckle, which provided me with even more motivation for me to deliver. As I had achieved "buy in" at every level as to what was expected of each team member, including buy in from the stakeholders we needed to support us, and the support of my family to do whatever I needed to do, I knew this was going to be nailed on ... and it was.

Six months later I shared my results alongside a superimposed picture of a red bus on the moon! It would have never happened without buy in, and of course, the heckle!

Inspiration—Of the leaders that I have worked with, the ones who have the ability and desire to be inspired themselves also demonstrate the same desire to inspire others.

It's like flour and eggs, you can't bake a cake without the other. Without fail, leaders who inspire others demonstrate a passion and love for whatever it is that they do. Inspirational people always display high energy, and it's that energy that captures our attention.

The reason why our heads are turned when we hear or see this is that, sadly, it's not as commonplace as we may first think in the business community. Have you heard the saying, "confidence is attractive?" Well, those who inspire others are riddled with confidence—it oozes from them in everything that they say and do. So when you are attracted, you are also likely to listen.

That's not all. Those who inspire us can often do so by using their knowledge and understanding of their subject matter. This can be demonstrated in sports, business, charities and at home. Others then realize that they too can achieve what their leaders are demonstrating. Yes, that's right, demonstrating. This is where the phrase "leading by example" is most relevant.

Our role as leaders is to inspire others to take action by showing them what's possible. Nelson Mandela was jailed for his beliefs for anti-apartheid campaigning in South Africa in 1964. He was the same man with the same passion and beliefs in jail. Keeping him in jail was the way in which the South African government dealt with suppressing his power and influence, and to reduce the likelihood of inspiring change in others.

Of course, once free from prison in 1990, it is well documented the lengths he took to show his followers what he would do. He subsequently inspired the nation and became President in 1994 in the country's first ever, multiracial elections; the rest is history.

Can you imagine Steve Jobs, the late CEO of Apple, Inc. inspiring others on conference calls and in e-mails from his ivory office tower? Of course not, he was the guy who was in each department, showing and sharing his wisdom, learning as much as he was teaching. Who did the product launch? Steve Jobs. Why? So he could inspire his clients and his staff alike that they were part of something bigger than just working for a company that made phones and computers.

His approach and results just didn't inspire Apple, but an entire industry. Indeed, he inspired the way in which we as a human race communicate in the twenty-first century. Test it ... ask whoever you are with or who you can phone, "Do you have an Apple product?" If they don't, ask "Do you know somebody who does?" The answers will probably either be, "Yes" or "No" and "Yes."

A final thing to think about is that inspiration is personal; you don't have to be a rock star, business head or an elite sports person. We can all be inspired by seeing anybody stretch, achieve and deliver an outstanding result for themselves. Simply being the best you can is the best you can deliver. If you deliver your very best, it can't get much better than that.

"Authentic leaders provide inspiration, but are also inspired themselves ... and so the cycle continues."
—Steve Rush

A Spoonful Too Much of Authenticity

I've had to think long and hard about this one, because authenticity provides many more benefits to support your *Cake* and help you on your business journey than it provides limitations. It then leads me to think of a leader I worked with who thought he was "authentic" and subsequently overplayed his attempt at authenticity by telling people of his originality, his uniqueness and so on. While he may well have been, that old social instinct in us starts to tell us, "If he was so genuine, then why is he telling us?" Authenticity should *show*, so there is no need to *tell*.

He was almost trying too hard to build affinity and rapport. As such, you never really got to see the soul of the individuals he worked with. It was always *his* focus, *his* agenda; and he only showed his people what *he* wanted them to see.

In my experience of coaching leaders, many leaders have well-formed, strong skill sets. It's a fine line where they overplay those strengths and then their strengths become their development areas too.

There is an enemy in authentic leadership: it is called, "Maverick." For those of you old enough to remember, it has nothing to do with the movie *Top Gun*. When you lead people, teams, and businesses, the word to focus on is "lead" them!

Often leaders become passionate, excited and driven to take their business in a different direction. Some leaders have already started work on the vision and strategy as soon as the thoughts have entered their brain and before they can communicate it.

There may be a place for maverick behavior in business in such activities as creating ideas and thinking outside the box. The definition means, *"one who does not conform,"* so if in crisis or urgency you need a quick thinking approach, the actions need to be aligned to your vision, values and goals. Conformity in this sense is when your approach does not support your vision, values and goals. Keep an eye out for mavericks in your behavior and that of your teams, as they have been known to ruin reputation and brand value in an instant.

Developing a sense of urgency is crucial in making change happen. A leader's role is to lead from the front with all of the subcomponent members of staff, stakeholders and clients following with you—or even stronger—amongst you. If you are able to create the right environment where the physical corporate hierarchy is no longer an issue, you will create greater affinity with people who can themselves have empathy at the pace at which you are working. Too much pace could cause people to have a lack of understanding and clarity at the direction of travel you are trying to achieve. This often appears to stray from urgency to panic. Panic is a bitter ingredient to have in your *Cake*.

A Spoonful Too Few of Authenticity

Have you ever left a meeting and the message or plans were a little "wishy washy." It is probably because you have something missing in your thinking. You may have observed somebody continually saying yes to their colleagues or their boss only to be seen as contradicting themselves or going with the consensus. As a leader, if you surround yourself with people who behave like this, you are at risk of losing credibility. This can subsequently impact your authenticity.

CASE STUDY Nigella was my boss; we used to call her the smiling assassin. She had developed the knack of giving unpleasant feedback while smiling all the way through a roasting or a telling off! It was such a shame. On the face of it, her *Cake* was really well baked.

To observers, she appeared to have the perfect recipe. She had charm, results, and she knew her business really well. It wasn't until you took a bite of her *Leadership Cake* that you realized that her *Cake* was missing an ingredient. You guessed it; she had just a spoonful too few of authenticity, but that was enough.

I had a number of conversations that involved her changing her mind and being very inconsistent in her actions. Her messages were often framed, "I know you may not want to do this and I tend to agree with you, but just do it!"

The pleasant messages were hers; the unpalatable messages were her bosses or some other co-worker. The impact this had on my peers and I was that over time we began to lose respect. A theme developed where a lack of trust started to creep in amongst us. Individuals were not supporting the vision in a way that they could.

Nigella's way of dealing with this was to smile ... always. So when things were good, she'd smile. When things were bad, she would still smile, which contradicted the severity of the tough conversation.

* * * *

When you can see, hear and feel somebody is being disingenuous, you become weary of what his/her true agenda is. They are not authentic and they lose impact as a leader.

Having a spoonful too few of authenticity in your *Cake* will leave a bad taste in your team's mouth.

I learned a very simple approach in my leadership career on this one: smile if you are happy, and don't if you are sad! Because being true to those around you is more important to others than how you want to be perceived.

Leaders who have such strong desire to be liked tend not to develop sustainable results. Leaders who have such strong desire to develop results tend not to be liked. Authenticity helps provide a balance between the two.

Take a moment to reflect on your authenticity as a leader and use the recipe pad on the following page to fine tune your "A" Authentic ingredients. Make sure you "add according to taste" what you need and "leave out" where you believe it may overpower your Cake.

Recipe Pad
"A" Authenticity

Add in ...

Leave out ...

Knowledge

In meetings and boardrooms, you may have heard that "knowledge is power." Well knowledge is only powerful if you or your business share that knowledge.

Occasionally when somebody has more knowledge than others, it can create a sense of technical hierarchy. In every organization, the broader the distribution of each member of staff's knowledge, the better equipped the organization can be at responding with agility to different situations and scenarios.

Knowledge is a core ingredient in your *Cake*. It has to be carefully measured out in order to complement communication, authenticity and empathy. As a leader, you don't have to be the subject matter expert. That is not what your knowledge is about.

To be as effective as you can, you will need a large range of information and knowledge at your finger tips if you want to improve results.

This means demonstrating to your direct reports sufficient information to be able to fully understand their business and communicate this knowledge effectively to the people you lead. It supports authenticity and empathy and is the perfect balancing ingredient in your *Leadership Cake*. It becomes easier for people to trust someone who understands them and their business.

Unlocking this knowledge from your organization will be a bi-product of a well-baked *Cake*. So how do you get your business to share the collective knowledge pool?

In my attempt to learn about the business areas that I led, I implemented a few simple activities that also helped me develop my *Cake* along the way. I was cognizant of the fact I needed to complement the other ingredients of communication, authenticity and empathy. An initiative I lead was called, "LTY," or listen to you forums. This was a platform for me to share my knowledge of the business, provide some direction, reinforce my vision and most importantly learn at various levels of my business all at the same time.

It was my chance to learn emotionally how my team and their teams were feeling, behaving and responding.

This was also a great opportunity for me to "fact find" and gather information from those experts in my business in order for me to understand more about the people that worked with me and gain more personal knowledge about key business areas.

During these forums I was also able to share my authenticity and communication. I couldn't guess what was going on, so by being amongst them, I could understand and build empathy with their position and at the same time improve my knowledge of the business.

I sponsored several initiatives as a leader of a business where technical knowledge seemed more fashionable than results. The staff collected professional qualifications like military personnel gained stripes and buttons on their uniforms. One such initiative was called "lunch & learn." It is a process where an open invitation was made weekly to the whole business to attend a talk or workshop run by a subject matter expert (SME) from a differing business unit. The SME presented, talked or trained about an element of their own business area during lunch break.

The results were great. The collective sharing of knowledge and ideas helped pull inter-division business areas together creating a coalition-like approach to our goals. It fostered inter-team communication and also helped people plan a career path that may not have been visible to them before this sharing took place.

As a leader and leader of leaders, my senior team and I were able to learn personally about key areas of our business.

"Knowledge Bank" was the term I used to capture two key areas of insight. The main objective of knowledge bank was to understand common issues and to allow our internal knowledge and expertise to naturally flow. I used a chat room format via our intranet, which a dedicated member of the team facilitated. It was self-managing. I had carefully communicated its objectives and positioned this carefully with the wider business. In my experience, if people have the answer and they feel confident in the environment to share it, they will. These initiatives were all great "windows on my world" and it allowed me to learn as much as I was able to teach.

A Spoonful Too Much of Knowledge

Where you observe an individual who believes knowledge is power, take a close interest. Two things are apparent when your technical experts believe that they have power from their knowledge. The first is that they strive to know more than anybody else in an attempt to self promote their technical value and appear to become almost indispensable. The second is that they adopt a selfish approach to self-development, which becomes more important to them than their business performance. Having experienced many a character like this, they may be amongst some of the least productive members of your team. Caution required!

Leadership requires you have knowledge. An old boss said to me as I journeyed into my first leadership role, "Steve, you will need to know it all—100%; however, you will probably need to use only 5% at a time, but what you won't know is which 5%."

It was a message that stayed with me through my career in my restless pursuit to know what I needed to know.

Leading with a spoonful too much of knowledge could be seen by your reports as your safety blanket. If your *Cake* is heavy with knowledge, it will not taste right. It may be seen as a weakness rather than a strength, and of course, it will not be in balance with your other ingredients and could overpower them.

Some of the leaders I have worked with even used their knowledge to deflect business issues. It's also been the case that they perceive the need to continue to grow knowledge, when it's the skills that need development.

Chinese philosopher, Lao-Tzu said:

"People find it difficult to govern because they have too much knowledge."

If we know it all as curious and progressive leaders, we then won't ask those critical and stretching questions we often need to ask to get an appropriate change in behavior and results. Questions are leadership food!

A Spoonful Too Few of Knowledge

Having a lack of knowledge in your *Cake* will make it taste bland. We explored that by having too much knowledge you could create an overplayed strength as a leader of an organization. Surely then the opposite would fix that problem, right? Not so. Your ingredients must be in the right proportion to have the appropriate effect or result. In my time coaching leaders with too few ingredients, we identified a development area. When a leader has a strong presence or too much of one ingredient, this becomes an overplayed strength and, again, an area of development.

So what characteristics would you expect your *Cake* to take on if there was not enough knowledge ingredient? Well, as a leader, your staff will look to you for confirmation and reassurance from time to time. You may recall that this is not about being a subject matter expert, but having enough knowledge to be credible.

Credibility appears as a balancing agent in some of the four key ingredients in your *Cake*, including knowledge. If you lack knowledge, you may lack credibility, which will undoubtedly also impact on your other ingredients such as authenticity and communication.

I recall working with a colleague called James. He was my "oppo." He ran the other division that mirrored mine in a large global business. I often took the opportunity to work with other leaders to observe what they did in order to help improve my own knowledge and awareness of the business. On this one particular day, we had to communicate some important changes in our operating model to our direct reports. Between them they made up the national leadership team.

We had divided the meeting and presentation in half and agreed between us what elements we would each lead. It is important when delivering a message with a co-worker to agree on a protocol of not involving ourselves in each other's session. This demonstrates respect to each other and a cohesive approach (as we did on this occasion). We had cascaded a large proportion of the day when James took to his feet once more.

He looked uncomfortable this time, almost nervous. I had not observed this in James, either earlier in the day or the previous time spent working together. The mood seemed to change somewhat and the tone and confidence in James' demeanor was obviously slipping. It was clear to me that James' *Cake* had a spoonful too few of knowledge and immediately the social instincts of the team smelled his *Cake* was not baked well at this time and they were keen to let him know. James had not done his homework, and despite having the time to familiarize himself with the information and call on subject matter experts to help in his briefing, he took the view that he had enough.

He lost credibility as fast as a trained chef could slice an apple. He created unease amongst our audience, which also raised questions about his leadership and indeed his integrity and authenticity. We closed our session having answered all of the outstanding questions raised. I watched with intrigue at the repair job that James created. It took some time to rebuild credibility with his team.

It taught me that even just a spoonful too little of knowledge in my *Leadership Cake* could unsettle the other ingredients and spoil the recipe for success.

Take a moment to reflect on your knowledge as a leader and use the recipe pad on the following page to fine tune your "K" Knowledge ingredients. Make sure you "add according to taste" what you need and "leave out" where you believe it may overpower your Cake.

Recipe Pad
"K" Knowledge

Add in ...

Leave out ...

Empathy

Empathy in your *Leadership Cake* acts as the eggs in regular cake. It binds the ingredients together and helps everything else stick together. A formal definition of empathy according to the *Oxford* dictionary is: "the power of identifying oneself mentally with (and so fully comprehending/understanding) a person or object of contemplation." Dr. Stephen Covey, author of the *7 habits of highly effective people* noted in habit number five (which has now become a well versed maxim), *"seek first to understand and then to be understood."*

It will come as no surprise to you that without truly understanding the tasks, situations, and the people who create, execute and lead them, your own *Leadership Cake* is not a really a *Cake*. A cake without eggs will be heavy, dense and flat. It will break and crumble easily and not be very palatable. Much like your *Leadership Cake* may taste without empathy. It's ironic that empathy is an emotion that in past business eras was seen as a sign of weakness. It was seen as an emotion not appropriate in a strong leadership environment, but has become a key ingredient in Leadership and also in your basic *Cake* mix.

Our brain has two hemispheres that are programmed and defined to do different jobs. The two hemispheres are our left brain and right brain. The left brain is responsible for things such as strategy, thinking, detail and a lot of the practical things we do as humans. The right brain is where we experience emotion, feelings, and the ability to see the big picture; this is also where we develop empathy.

LEFT SIDE		**RIGHT SIDE**
Logic		Feelings
Facts		Intuition
Detail		Emotions
Numbers		Pictures
Words		Sensing
Planning		Risk taking
Complexity		Nonverbal
Decisions		Big Picture

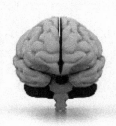

Where this irony continues is that all through our childhood and into our adult life, we are broadly taught using the left thinking side of our brain. Let's just explore this for a moment. As children we were taught structures such as the alphabet, our times tables, mathematic equations and formulas. Then when it came to examinations, we were instructed to study, learn verbatim, and whilst in the exam situation, to regurgitate this into answers. This is all left brain thinking.

Therefore I surmise that it's not surprising that the students who had a more dominant left side of their brain achieved the best results. These same individuals were also awarded the better college places, repeated the regurgitation and as a result had better degrees and ultimately secured more senior positions. These more senior roles allow decision making in business at a level where often the right-brained dominant leaders are less apparent.

Since empathy is right brain thinking, this could be why some leaders still show little empathy.

One hypothesis is that they have been working their left brain for so long, it may be more dominant than their right side, and that the emotional side of understanding people is thus harder to grasp than that of naturally dominant right brain thinkers.

It's also true that some people who leave school with no qualifications and no apparent chances have become some of the most successful entrepreneurs. Where opportunity played into their path during their adult life, they could fully explore and utilize their right brain thinking. Having a clear dollop of empathy in their *Cake* would almost be a surety.

Laurence Graff tops the "no qualifications vocational rich list" with a personal wealth of over $4.3 billion built on an international diamond business. He spent his first seven years in a single room in Whitechapel, East London, England shared with his Jewish Orthodox parents. At thirteen, Graff left school early and took on a Hatton Garden apprenticeship in the diamond trade. He began buying and selling stones in 1957 and opened

Hatton Garden's first retail jeweler five years later at age twenty-four. By the mid-sixties, his store was regarded as a must be shop for the uber-rich.

So how do you know if you have a more dominant left or right brain? Well, I suspect in reading the last few pages, if you clung to every word then perhaps you are left brained. If you started to recognize yourself in the story, this suggests right brain thinking. Here's another way of telling. Have a look at the image below and write in the box on the right the first thing you see:

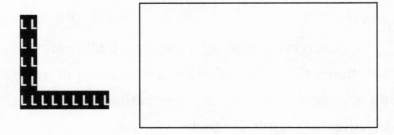

If you have written that you saw, "a group of the letter Ls," this suggests that you are more dominant in left brain thinking. You are drawn more to the detail. If you saw, "the shape of a letter L," this suggests you are more of a right brain thinker.

All leaders need to be aware of their natural dominance so they can develop their thinking accordingly. Those leaders who are able to share information between hemispheres in their brain are likely to be more successful and generally have a better balance in their thinking. These leaders can dive into detail, but remain emotionally aware, and can also see the bigger picture.

So whilst empathy exists more readily in right brain thinkers, it needs to be a core ingredient in our entire *Leadership Cake* recipe. We will explore your recipe shortly and the effects of having a spoonful too much or a spoonful too few of empathy.

There is an adage: if you want to understand what it's like from another's point of view, "walk in their shoes for a day." In other words, manage to step into their position and observe the scenario from another individuals' perspective.

Here is my checklist to help develop empathy.

- Build affinity
- Actively listen
- Let them have their say
- Ask lots of questions
- Put on their shoes
- Let them know you know

Build affinity. The more you have in common with people, the more you naturally get along with people. You have heard the saying, "birds of a feather, flock together?" So how do you build and develop affinity? It's about finding out as much about the other person as possible. One way to get information is to give information first, such as family hobbies, and then ask, "so what about you?" Your role as an effective communicator is to then identify what synergies exist and share that common ground. The better affinity you have with another, the easier it is to understand and empathize with them.

Actively listen. By using your right brain, you can demonstrate to another that you are listening and have heard what has been said. Use positive nodding gestures, maintain eye contact and play back what you have heard. This demonstrates you have listened and understood what they have said.

You may recall from earlier in the book where we explored "C" in *Cake*, that the person you are communicating with will also be communicating with you using nonverbal messages. Thus, grasping the unspoken word is an essential balancing ingredient to help develop empathy.

Let them have their say. Let them go and let them vent. Many of our initial reactions are wrapped in a parcel of emotion; interpreting that is a skill. Don't be tempted to interrupt, as this initial reaction can be full of clues as to the root cause of what you are hearing or seeing. Often our emotional reactions provide ill thought through responses; however, they can help build an understanding as to what an individual has on their mind.

That's a good thing. If you know what the issues are, you can deal with them. Getting things aired and in the open means as a leader you can demonstrate empathy and be more measured in your reaction with a team member, as you will be more informed.

Ask lots of questions. Once you know the issues, your next job is to explore them. What is the next question you should ask? ... No, I meant "WHAT" is the next question you should ask! Asking *what* questions really help you pin point information quickly and using *what* questions following additional *what* questions helps you explore and probe more effectively. Here's an example:

"What was the real issue with that? What specifically? The *what* question has an important role in removing emotion and helps separate desirable information from essential facts. Some leaders, when looking for an answer, will often ask, "Why is that an issue?" In asking a "Why" question you have a significant chance of getting a spurious response, such as, "I don't know," or "Just because it was," or "You tell me." Whereas, "What was the reason that was an issue for you?" in most cases would more likely give you the reason rather than an emotional response.

Put on their shoes. There is an old proverb: "To understand a man, you've got to walk a mile in his shoes, whether they fit or not."

As a leader, if you second guess or get feedback from others and take an educated guess at another's point of view, your *Leadership Cake* will struggle as your "E" Empathy ingredients will not be right. The only way to truly understand is by getting in amongst it, leading with visibility and example by demonstrating a desire to truly learn what it's like for the people you lead.

Let them know you know. The final step in the empathy checklist is to share what you have observed and witnessed. Show them that you truly understand their position—good, bad and indifferent. You get it, or not as the case may be. I call this "Playback," where you playback everything you have heard. Often as leaders, this may mean playing back unpalatable feedback and things you will need to be accountable for. This has nothing to do with showing signs of weakness, on the contrary. Playing back their words supported with additional context and helping their thinking to support your understanding is important.

Context X Understanding = Empathy

Ever messed up as a leader? It happens. If you mess up, saying sorry can be a wonderful gesture that demonstrates humility. Letting them know you have messed up can ensure they develop empathy for your journey too, in much the same was as you will have developed empathy for theirs.

Empathy vs. Sympathy

Before we finish baking a balanced yet basic *Leadership Cake*, don't take the *Cake* out of the oven too late. If you do, it may spoil. Sympathy is what happens when you leave your *Cake* baking for too long. Empathy is essential; sympathy can be disastrous. The best way to explain this is using the little example below:

Sympathy ...

Is about when you see a team member in a hole and you jump in with them.

Now you are part of the problem.

Empathy ...

Is about throwing them a ladder and helping them out.

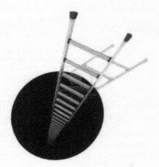

Now you are part of the solution.

Take a moment to reflect on your Empathy as a leader and use the recipe pad on the following page to fine tune your "E" Empathy ingredients. Make sure you "add according to taste" what you need and "leave out" what you believe may overpower your Cake.

Recipe Pad
"E" Empathy

Add in ...

Leave out ...

3 *Let Them Eat Cake*

So now you have a well-formed and risen *Leadership Cake*. For those who experience your *Cake*, it should be palatable and appetizing with a good blend of core ingredients including: Communication, Authenticity, Knowledge and Empathy at the heart of its creation.

From here on in you can now develop your career as a leader knowing full well that your foundation or base level is well placed to inspire and take your team and results to the next level. This is just the start as there is more work to be done to ensure your *Cake* continues to be appealing.

Many leaders, having developed their leadership style either by luck or by judgment, simply stop at this point. While your *Cake* may taste just great right now, you can bet that some other leader's *Cake* has a nice juicy filling or lovely sweet icing that could tempt your most trusted and loyal staff away from you and your business. This chapter explores that your fruity or creamy filling is a metaphor for personal development and this is in the very center of your *Cake*. Sharing your *Leadership Cake* with your team will help create a great, memorable experience and provide a differentiator between leaders.

Another trait demonstrated by great leaders is that they all are agile enough to develop and adapt in a changing world. Not only are they able to adapt their business acumen to the commercial world they operate in, they also demonstrate an ability to grow their knowledge, skills and capabilities.

A bi-product of this leadership agility and self-awareness in developing themselves is that they also keep hold of the team of individuals that they lead—their direct reports. Great teams share consistency and longevity as they grow together. They learn from one another about the strengths they each possess. With the same agile leadership, the leader is able to maximize the team dynamics by playing to those strengths and capitalizing on the experience and styles of each team member.

Based on my research and in my experience, the greatest gift any leader can give is the gift of learning.

Developing your team is a sure fire way of retaining and indeed recruiting talented people. This is also where leaders will need to be bold. It is inevitable that if we do sponsor the development of others, *Leadership Cake* in their own right may match or even become greater, more appetizing than your own, and that's a good thing.

In my leadership career, I was privileged to lead some dedicated and eager team members. It thrilled me immensely to see these bright, energetic individuals develop and receive career progression and even leave my team and business as a result. The reason it provided me with real satisfaction was that we did it together, and it was planned and managed with no shocks. That is critical in the planning process of any team.

It would have been a different experience if these same individuals had left my service simply because they were able to get a better tasting *Leadership Cake* experience elsewhere. When it comes to making your *Cake* taste better than other leaders, developing yourself and others creates a healthy environment and will set you apart from the rest.

How can your own development make your *Cake* taste better? I concluded that for those leaders who were open and responsive to self-development these same leaders were also as equally keen to develop the people around them. This creates a

culture where a restless curiosity for training, learning and improvement become business as usual. If you were given the choice to work with a leader who had personal development running through them versus another who showed no appetite for development, whom would you rather work with? It isn't such a big choice is it? But ironically, many leaders in business have adopted a selfless philosophy that the learning and development activities should be for their team and staff rather than themselves.

I have written to over 500 business leaders and established that their main source of development is broadly based on self-help books, blogs and journals. This is a great idea and I thoroughly recommend reading as part of any self-development strategy.

All good leaders should continue to read with a view to improve—after all, you wouldn't be reading this now if that wasn't a good idea, right? However, the problem with self-help is that it's all down to you. If you immerse yourself with your team's development, not only do you learn while you lead together, but you also ensure your core *Cake* ingredients maintain their structure.

Another finding is that a large number of leaders and executives have the, "I don't know what I should develop in" syndrome. When I coach leaders and I hear this, I suggest that the first element on their personal development and coaching plan should be "self awareness." It's a stark reality that many spend so much time focusing on developing others and running their business, that the one person who is often the rainmaker or the glue of the organization doesn't develop themselves effectively.

There are two other key factors to consider for leaders who have a less fruity, thin and flavorless filling:

1)   They invariably stop asking for feedback.

2)   They create a culture whereby people
       don't feel comfortable providing feedback
       to the boss for fear of reprisal.

Either way, this contributes to a lack of self-awareness and an understanding of what they should be doing to improve themselves and others.

A lack of filling will create a less appetizing *Leadership Cake*; in fact it will eventually turn their *Cake* stale. What was once a fluffy sponge will turn hard and disheveled as it will sit uneaten on the *Leadership Cake* stand while *Cake* lovers look for fresher and better baked *Cake* to experience.

It is in significant contrast to those leaders whose *Cake* filling is brimming at the edges, loaded with fresh appetizing personal development. As a leader with strong development principles, your eagerness to take your newly acquired skills, knowledge and information back to the workplace will not only help you embed new behaviors yourself, but your business will be the direct beneficiary of the ripple effect.

The learning culture becomes infectious as your direct reports, peers and others around you will see and feel the improved energy that comes along with doing something new and different. In addition to the improvement in your results, your business growth will be sustainable too.

In today's technology driven world, there is no excuse for not making sure your filling is brimming. The introduction of the Internet and Cloud means that learning can be accessed not only through books, articles or blogs, but also through mediums such as webinars, e-learning modules, online classrooms, YouTube videos and seminars as well as social media sites. You can access all of these from your office desk.

Understanding your learning style is really important condiment in your *Cake*. If you attempt to undertake a learning event that doesn't suit your style, you will not get the best outcome. There are many written processes and models designed to help you understand your preferred learning style. I assume you are already reasonably aware of what you like, but the following table may help you reframe what works best for you.

Learning Style	Model/Process
I prefer to see	Video, e-learning Online classrooms Face-to-Face / Live Events
I prefer to hear	Audio books, CDs, MP3, Podcasts
I prefer to be involved	Face-to-Face Seminars, Live Events, Workshops, Coaching

Leaders also learn from other leaders, so I would very much encourage as much networking as you can possibly fit into your busy schedule. Social media is great, but many local organizations and associations exist solely to promote getting together. As part of these events, you are not only exposed to leaders who have a variety of *Cakes*, but they often invite guest speakers to these events who have the best of the best *Cakes* in the *Cake* shop.

 Mark and Sally both started their leadership journey together. They had good sponsorship from their organization and attended their initial leadership development program three years ago. They have the exact same number of team members and also have the same demography in their business areas.

Every day they applied similar disciplines and behaviors learned from the outset via their development program. They recruited well in the early years and both were excited at the prospect of leadership.

Mark was a great communicator. He was measured in his approach and his understanding of the levels of knowledge was strong enough to maintain and explore the strengths and challenges within his team. He had modeled good behavior from other leaders, but had his own personal style that was trusted by his team. Mark's *Leadership Cake* had a strong foundation, as all of the four core ingredients were present.

Sally was very unique in her approach to leading others. She had studied hard to fill her knowledge gaps and spent a significant amount of time working and collaborating with her direct reports to understand how it was for them in their roles and work area. She was very aware not to bombard them with lots of information and she was applauded for her communication style. Sally's *Leadership Cake* also had all of the core ingredients.

During year three at the midyear board meeting while presenting their first six months results, reality started to dawn on Mark.

Despite the apparent parity between the two teams, the performance gap on measures such as results, recruitment, attrition and staff engagement had started to widen faster than the jaws of a yawning lion, and his team was the bottom jaw.

Sally had no staff retention issues; in fact she had such a strong pipeline of new potential recruits she found herself in the position of having to stand down the recruitment agency's search activity. She had very little attrition within her team. During the last six months, only one team member had left her service; he now sat next to Mark as a peer in the same board meeting. Her staff engagement was the highest in the business, some ten points ahead of Mark's team. Her business results had improved month on month and while Mark still had good results, his team's last six months were the poorest since he took up his position. To add insult to injury, two of his most productive team players had just left. One for a competitor and another had asked for a transfer. How could this be? His *Cake* had all the right core ingredients.

Mark was a good guy; he had the makings of a great leader, but he had been so caught up with the day-to-day running of his business that he had not spent any time developing either his personal or career learning goals. Mark was still unclear, "how and what it was," that was making such a difference in Sally's team effectiveness.

No sooner as the meeting had finished, he whisked Sally to the coffee shop across the street quicker than a hot knife could pass through ice cream.

Mark was anxious, "Sally, you have to tell me, what is it you're doing to get such great results?"

She paused for a minute. "Well, I have the same operating platform, products and facilities as you do. I had the same education, training and sponsorship as you. What feedback have you received from your team, Mark?" She asked nonchalantly.

Mark hesitated before answering as he had a moment of self-reflection. "I haven't really asked for feedback. I've been very close to the business, and the team is always open with me. I believe they share everything I need, but I haven't asked! Darn it... how foolish of me!" he yelled.

It was at that moment that Mark realized that he was too deep in his business and had become unaware of the impact to his team and what they needed in a leader. He had not spent time considering how he was performing and had made assumptions about his people and their needs. Most significant of all was there wasn't a culture of development in either him or his team.

Mark's *Cake* was sound, but his filling was bland and tasteless. Even though Mark's overall approach was good, this became too mundane for many of his team. Some found that they could get a better tasting *Leadership Cake* with other departments and other businesses, which would eventually hit the bottom line results.

In contrast, Sally had placed a significant focus on developing herself. She had a well thought through personal learning plan that helped her manage her work-based activities while also focusing on her development. Her philosophy to personal development was evident at the heart of everything she did.

Having been recognized by the business as a leader who was keen to develop her effectiveness and progress in the organization, Sally's learning and development activities had a positive impact on her team. Much of the learning she undertook focused on her skills and behaviors. She transferred newly acquired skills and knowledge to her role, thus both Sally and her direct reports were the beneficiaries. Another physical effect of her passionate approach to her development was that it became infectious within her team. Her direct reports resonated with her messages and activities, and were inspired to develop themselves.

The outcome of this was that Sally was able to retain and develop a talented team, attract great quality candidates to backfill those who were promoted or left because their values didn't fit into her team ethic. Staff felt supported and engaged, which was notable in her business results and staff opinion poll.

Sally's *Leadership Cake* was oozing with bright energetic filling. She was attracting the right behavior and results because she recognized that if she wanted to be noticed, her filling or personal development needed to stand out and make her more appealing than other leaders.

* * * *

Picture the scene: you have two job offers to consider. Both jobs pay the same salary; they have an equal benefits package. The organization and the career progression appear identical. You have just finished the recruitment process and meet with the two new prospective bosses. One has a strong development culture and the other does not. This would appear to you as two *Cakes* on a cake stand: one has as a heap of fresh fruit and cream, and the other a thin layer of butter. You get to choose!

That's how different you could look if your *Leadership Cake* is absent of a great filling with personal development running through the heart of it.

Take a moment to reflect on the filling in your Cake, your self-development as a leader. Use the recipe pad on the following page to fine tune the ingredients in your "Filling." Make sure you "add according to taste" what you need and "leave out" where you believe it may overpower your Cake.

Recipe Pad
Filling

Add in ...

Leave out ...

4 *Icing on the Cake*

When you visit an artisan cake shop and you look at the array of cakes on display, you'll find an enormous variety to choose from. Even if you observed a few cakes that looked the same on the outside, there are subtle differences that make them unique.

As a Leader, it's the subtle differences that make you stand out in the corporate *Cake* shop. It's the same subtle differences that make you more appealing to the eye than other *Cakes* or leaders, and that is down to you, how you carry yourself and what you want others to see.

In this chapter, I will explore the external view of your *Cake*, and the reasons that somebody may select your *Leadership Cake* over another's. Your external brand follows the same principle as when you visit the baker's shop: cakes are decorated with icing, candy sprinkles, fruit and cream, etc. This does two things.

First, it catches your eye and looks appetizing, which makes you want that cake. Second, it lets you know what it is—it tells you it is a cream sponge, or a chocolate fudge brownie or a baked cheesecake, etc.

Over time you may have developed an eye to recognize certain cakes without even tasting it in the baker's shop. You'll know which cake it is and what it may taste like based purely on what you can see, smell and have experienced in the past.

The icing on your *Leadership Cake* is what is on display and your boss or potential boss, peers and co-workers will make a quick judgment based on what they see and smell from you and your icing.

So when I refer to icing, I want you to think of yourself as the well formed *Cake* that has been put together and baked with care and that your icing is what others can see. Let's put it another way, what is it you stand for? What are the visible values and beliefs you display openly? What you are about? What does your icing actually say about your *Leadership Cake*?

Icing = Your Personal Brand

The reason it is important to be clear about your icing is that people will decide whether or not to try your *Leadership Cake* on appearance first and taste second. If you think of a time where you selected a new employer, you will have undoubtedly met with your new boss at some point during the selection process before you agreed to take that position. You may have had several meetings with them, but it's highly likely that you would have only experienced their icing by this stage.

It is unlikely you would have had the opportunity to taste their *Leadership Cake* until you were in role (unless you had prior experience with them). In some organizations where mentoring is encouraged as part of a developmental strategy, you may be able to taste other's *Leadership Cake*s and compare what you may like or dislike about other leaders. You may even start formulating an opinion about the type of *Cake* you may want in a prospective leader. After all, what would stop you from exploring or even asking for their recipe or a sample tasting?

My counsel to any new recruit would be to communicate with those who have already tasted the *Cake*; they will tell you what that was like for them. (Caution required: we all have different palates, or likes and dislikes of different flavors, so while this is important, it should only form part of your research, not all of it.)

It's often true that until you have eaten the icing and tasted the *Cake* underneath you don't truly realize the *Leadership Cake* within. Imagine a brightly decorated *Cake* with cream and cherries to boot, but inside you find a dry sponge, with hardly a trace of filling ... appetizing? I don't think so. Many leaders fall into this trap; they buy a sharp suit, classic handmade Italian shoes and wear an expensive Swiss wristwatch. They also appear to say the right things. These things may be important, but if the icing is just a front or a cover for a *Cake* that has a spoonful too much or too few of key ingredients, the effectiveness of that leader is compromised. It will become apparent that they lack core ingredients. If only they had the recipe, right?

From a very early age, we are bombarded with media that exposes us to brands. Marketers have come to the conclusion that the earlier you can create brand awareness in consumers, the more likely you are to recruit and retain their patronage and loyalty Over time, organizations have built and developed significant and well recognized brands that now are synonymous with what their product or service promises to deliver. To focus your mind on "brand," look about the room or office you are sitting in right now and see how many you can list in this box.

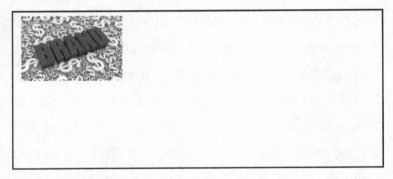

How different from the well-known corporate images and brands you listed in the previous box should your personal brand or icing be?

Initially, you need to be clear as to what you want your *Leadership Cake* to look like. What is it that you want to say to people with your icing? What is the story your brand will share at a glance?

In the personal brand awareness workshops that I run, I encourage my delegates to physically draw or describe their brand in order to help stimulate their thinking. I then ask, "Does this really describe you? And does this accurately reflect what you stand for?" What would your slogan or tagline say? Draw your *Cake* with the icing below (think *brand*). I'd like you to share what top three ingredients you would use in your icing/topping and condiments, and what those ingredients say about you. Try it—have some fun with it, you may be surprised what you discover when you really think, "I'm a *Leadership Cake* in a cake shop."

For example, here's my *Cake*:

 The creamy whipped icing represents a fresh balanced exterior that may be overpowering if consumed in large quantities. The mixed fruit and chocolate represents that each slice or experience may represent a different taste.

Now it's your turn.

Your icing or topping ingredients

1)..

Represents...........................

....

2)..

Represents...........................

....

3)..

Represents...........................

....

Once you are really clear as to what your icing is, how can you ensure that the *Leadership Cake* you have crafted is really what it appears to be, or that your brand is an accurate reflection of who and what you stand for?

As leaders, we need to do more of this, and it's not a science: the answer is "ask for feedback." The great news is that by the time you even think icing, your *Leadership Cake* has already got quality core ingredients supporting what you are and what you represent. The question to ask yourself is: "Does my personal brand support my leadership style and is it congruent?" Congruence in this instance means that if we were to cut into your *Leadership Cake* beyond your icing or personal brand, would what people see be aligned with what they experience from the other parts of your *Leadership Cake*?

This will be more apparent to those who work with you and have already experienced a blend of Communication, Authenticity, Knowledge and Empathy. If your icing is appealing to the eye and is a fair reflection of your intent, you will not be on the *Leadership Cake* stand for long. Conversely, if you haven't gotten it right, word will soon get out. If the icing and the *Cake* look fantastic, but the taste doesn't live up to the recipient's expectations, you may find yourself sitting in the *Leadership Cake* shop a long time. Then, they may decide your kind of *Cake* is no longer right for the market you are operating in.

Feedback will help you understand if you are congruent with what you do, say and how you appear. It may lead you to re-think and adapt your icing or branding.

Brands change. If you look at some strong, long-lasting brands, you'll notice that while they may still hold their corporate values and messages, these brands have adapted over time to reflect current trends and market conditions.

You may need to adapt and add to your ingredients in baking your *Leadership Cake*. Like corporate brands, being aware of external factors, markets and attitudes is important in your brand and icing too. Brand awareness will ensure that you fly out of the *Cake* shop.

Take a moment to reflect on the icing on your Cake, your personal brand as a leader. Use the recipe pad on the following page to fine you're your "icing." Make sure you "add according to taste" what you need and "leave out" where you believe it may overpower your Cake.

Recipe Pad
Icing

Add in ...

Leave out ...

108

5 *Crumbs & All—The Aftertaste*

When you've eaten cake; all that is left are the crumbs. What was it that made you enjoy it— how it made you feel maybe? Certainly how it tasted. Our taste buds are covered in between 2,000 and 8,000 tiny receptors that tell us if the taste was bitter, sweet or sour. These receptors send information to the brain and it's our brain that deciphers that information and provides us with an experience.

You create the same experience and effect when the people who follow you have tasted your *Leadership Cake*. If their experience was a sweet one, they may use that part of their brain to recall those emotions and feelings to remember your *Cake* and the taste it left behind. It may provide them with thoughts of comfort and indeed shape their own recipe for their *Leadership Cake*.

You create experiences also if the taste of your *Cake* was a bitter or a sour one; the same recall may happen, but this time the taste would have been somewhat different and thus their memory of that time is unlikely to be positive.

We often have a perception that we must role model positive attributes and behavior. This approach helps us understand what good looks like, and I would agree. There is another hypothesis, and that is: we can learn equally from experiences both positive and negative. As a consultant or coach, I have found myself learning a lot from the impact a poor leader can have on their people and organization.

If we revisit the principles of *CAKE*, we may now understand that getting the right ingredients, and mixing them in the right way is not simply about how you lead at this moment.

How you lead and inspire (or not) in the future will leave an impression. Be mindful of your impact and your ingredients early on in your leadership career because it will shape the legacy you leave behind.

Having a well-prepared *Cake* with great filling and icing is not only important for attracting the right team, but for retaining that team as well.

The longer-lasting memory of your *Leadership Cake* builds your legacy as a leader. It becomes the aftertaste of your *Cake* and what they will remember you for.

I'm sure that if I asked you the following two questions, you could answer them without hesitation:

1) Who was the greatest leader you worked with?

2) Name the leader you least enjoyed working with?

Simply put, when all that is left behind are the crumbs, this is the aftertaste of their *Leadership Cake*. At that time, the experience hit your many receptors and you formed a reaction in your brain that was either positive or not so positive. Either way, you have an aftertaste, right?

Our legacy as leaders is all about the experience that our *Leadership Cake* provided to those who worked with us. Despite having attempted to create the most perfect, creative and tasty *Leadership Cake*, it's often not about the *Cake* you think you have made, and rarely how well you think your *Cake* was received, but instead it is what people are saying and sharing about your *Cake* that is critical in your leadership career. The impact you have directly with an individual will determine whether they spread good news or negative reviews. This will either help create a supportive message about your leadership, or a negative one that can be destructive and limiting.

CASE STUDY Ethan was a tyrant leader who was hotheaded, grumpy, and almost dictatorial in his approach. He ruled with an iron fist. His employee scores were outstanding, his results first class. Wait a minute: something's not right here is it? Ethan had created a day-to-day business culture where the people who experienced his *Cake* were so afraid to speak openly in fear of reprisal that they just got on with the job. The communication was an overpowering ingredient in his *Cake*—the empathy was so little. His staff saw him as aggressive and they were afraid of being honest and responding openly for fear of losing their jobs.

Staff plucked up courage to leave the business one by one, and slowly overtime felt free enough to say how it really was. This was the start of the end for Ethan; his legacy had started to build and it wasn't great.

In the local community where he was running his business, word was out: Ethan was a tyrant. "Don't work with that guy, he'll make your life hell," was often heard between fellow job hunters. Sadly, his *Cake* wasn't a good *Leadership Cake*, and the aftertaste was a bitter one.

Ethan's legacy was now folklore. Even people who had never worked with him or even met him had formed an opinion of who he was and how he did things based purely on the leadership legacy he left behind.

CASE STUDY Sophia was a firm but fair leader. She was operating a successful competitor firm a few blocks away from Ethan. Sophia had high standards, but aligned with clear expectations. Everybody knew that if they worked effectively, they would be rewarded handsomely. Equally, everybody knew that if they did not deliver on across balanced measures, then it was the highway for them. Her business was in a town where people would come and go. Staff turnover had been an ongoing issue for the business, yet recruitment and resourcing was always well planned, and they were able to fill their vacancies immediately.

Sophia also had a legacy. When those same job hunters asked, "What do you know about Sophia's business?" The response had some common themes that included: "She's really honest. You know where you stand with her," to "she understands the business and spends a lot of time with her people," and "everybody trusts her." Her *Cake* had all the core ingredients, she had a great approach to personal development, and she did and said what she believed in.

Despite having taken care of her own personal development and being aware of what else she needed to work on, she had created an authentic legacy in which people could recall a positive experience having worked in her firm. Over time she fine tuned her *Leadership Cake* ingredients and became even more effective. Her legacy became stronger and deeper ingrained in the same folklore that caused such problems for Ethan. People who had never worked with Sophia had formed an opinion based on the legacy she had created, and it was a positive one. Her legacy helped create an almost virtual marketing campaign in the local community that also helped support and build a growing and successful business.

* * * *

Some of the leaders we talked about in the opening chapter (Gandhi, Churchill, Welch, Branson and Gates) have a legacy that is unique to them. Legacies are developed by the shared experiences of others, not just the actions of the leaders themselves. These leaders' legacies were built by the followers and co-workers who openly and objectively recalled what their *Cakes* tasted like.

I made an interesting discovery during my research in response to the question, "Can you recall some great leaders of our time." Most individuals could recall somebody they knew based on what they observed of them and what others were saying about their *Leadership Cake*. It was less about their aftertaste. Where they were able to articulate a strong recollection, their aftertaste was generally very positive. Not many were able to explain what specific role, title or job they had held at the time. This tells me that experience is everything. The better the experience, the more recall they were able to re-introduce. The less positive experience, the less recall they could remember.

We discussed the power of the brain earlier. Researchers have identified that we are more likely to suppress or substitute unhappy or very uncomfortable memories because our brain processes those feelings differently. Thus, we have a natural tendency to recall positivity. This hypothesis supports that the better leaders who provide the better experience can create a snowball effect, growing momentum the longer that that success lasts, and developing a successful legacy in leadership.

It is important to remember that a great deal of learning can be derived from poor leaders and their ineffective approaches, as long as we process that experience by asking ourselves, "What did I learn from that experience?"

Having an acute awareness that "every day is a school day" and that learning is a positive thing is essential for developing your leadership legacy. If we view every experience as a learning event, we may not process it as an uncomfortable or bad experience at all.

If you apply the "learning approach" to any bad experience, it will help support your legacy, because others will be able to recall the positive learning experience derived despite the adverse situation.

We are more inclined to seek learning experiences if our brain recognizes them as positive and we will also be more receptive to those experiences in the future.

Ironically, those leaders who have buried, suppressed or substituted their previous bad or negative experiences tend to repeat that very same thing because they have forgotten what it felt like for them. Not recognizing the learning in adversity, which is broadly a positive connotation, will mean that the leader in those circumstances is left with a less positive outcome. So, their legacy or taste of their *Leadership Cake* is more likely to hit the sour and bitter taste receptors and leave an unpleasant aftertaste.

The best pastry chefs and master artisan bakers will spend hours researching ingredients, cooking techniques, products and methodologies. They also start this approach with, "When my customer has eaten my cake, how will it make them feel?"

Have you ever entered a project, event, board meeting or meeting with your team with the presence of mind that says something like, "I want them to feel valued, understood, trusted and appreciated and I want them to feel, I know how it is. I also get where they are and want them to know that I am there for them."?

If you have, that's fantastic, but do you do that every single time? When they have consumed your *Leadership Cake* and you're no longer in sight or available, that's all they have left, right?

By virtue of leading a business, this has to be commercially viable too, so having a commercial eye on the effects of your approach is essential.

What would make your people and others around you want to come back and experience some more of your *Cake* or indeed, try some of your other products? It is, of course, your legacy. You can argue with numbers and facts, but you can never argue with how you made them feel.

So, you have experienced getting the minimum core four ingredients and baking them to perfection. You also understand that you need to balance your ingredients: a spoonful too much or too few of these and your *Cake* is not a *Leadership Cake*, even if it may look like one.

Getting this part of the baking process right simply means that you have a great chance of becoming a great leader, but there is still work to do. Getting your filling right is essential to attracting, developing and retaining great staff too. Your *Cake* may thus be more appetizing than other leaders'; hence staff is more likely to choose you to lead them.

Your *Cake* speaks to who you are now, but your icing reflects the ongoing perception of others. Be careful and selective about what that says about you. If there were another you, looking back at you, what would you see?

 Careful planning of your *Cake* now will leave a lasting aftertaste forever. You are the master baker of your *Leadership Cake*. How well have you thought through your ingredients? Are you thinking about the present or your legacy?

Good luck in baking your *Leadership Cake*!

About the Author

Steve Rush

Steve is the CEO of Improov Consulting. Steve has had a successful Executive Leadership career with several global businesses where he was personally responsible for multi-million dollar revenue and billions of dollars of funds and assets.

He became a coach and business consultant to other executives to pass on his learning, studies and leadership lessons. Steve has experienced extremes of leadership styles: he has been lead by and has lead the good, bad and indifferent types of leaders. He now coaches, trains and supports leaders from junior level to international CEOs of global organizations.

After extensive research and testing of *Leadership Cake* "live" with leaders, their feedback has inspired him to share and develop the *Leadership Cake* philosophy. Of course, the proof is in the eating.

**Need more help with your
Leadership Development or developing
your personal recipe?**

Contact us now and find out about:

- *Leadership Cake* 360° Online Feedback
- *Leadership Cake* 360° One-on-One Coaching
- *Leadership Cake* Development Courses

www.leadershipcake.com

www.improovconsulting.com

@LeadershipCake @S_Rush_IMPROOV

http://lnkd.in/U8W9T

https://www.facebook.com/improov

Printed in the USA
CPSIA information can be obtained
at www.ICGtesting.com
LVHW091033060324
773720LV00001B/93